AF904529

You Know You're in a Toxic Relationship If . . .

(and How to Tell if You Are OUT of a Toxic Relationship)

by

Cage Riley, IV and Bunny Liberty

ISBN : Softcover 1-4134-8888-9

This book was printed in the United States of America.

To order additional copies of this book, contact:
Xlibris Corporation
1-888-795-4274
www.Xlibris.com
Orders@Xlibris.com
28281

DEDICATION

This book is dedicated to all those toxic people out there who have managed to make life miserable for so many of us. Even though you are all forgiven, that is no excuse for being such knuckleheads for so long to so many people who wanted to believe you were as nice as you said you were.

CONTENTS

PREFACE

Obviously, no one person can have all of the negative traits listed in this diminutive helpbook, yet many people we have talked to have been entangled in toxic relationships where they were controlled, intimidated, suffocated, frightened, and, yes, sometimes injured physically by individuals with many of the personality traits listed in this book.

All of the character traits in this book are a composite of a wide variety of people and people's personalities we have either experienced personally in toxic relationships we have been in over the course of our lives, or that have been shared with us by friends, co-workers, relatives, neighbors, and even that sad stranger lingering over the turnips at the supermarket.

Often in life, we humans are sucked unexpectedly into relationships that at the beginning look and feel great, only to have an "uh oh" kind of moment, when we realize that that "special someone" we have fallen for is not very special . . . and we start planning our escape.

Therefore, if you often say to yourself, "I would rather spend an evening dining on fava beans and sharing a nice bottle of Chianti with Hannibal Lecter than with that 'special someone' in my life," then read on . . .

PART ONE

You Know You're in a Toxic Relationship If . . .

. . . you are planning your escape from the relationship every waking minute, like a hamster planning its escape from its cage . . . and

. . . whenever you are in his/her company, he/she ALWAYS makes you feel bad about yourself.

Your friends' and family members' most frequently asked questions include:

1. *How many more years are you going to put up with his/her crap?*

2. *Have you read the latest book on toxic relationships?*

3. *Have you sent in your Dr. Phil tape yet?*

4. *Can I rent you a U-Haul?*

5. *Man/girl, when are you gonna get out of that situation?*

6. *Can I help you move? Get you boxes? Lend you money?*

7. *Do you want the name of a good lawyer or hitman?*

8. *Do you know that all of us—your friends, co-workers, family—ALL OF US—are as sick of him/her and your situation as you are AND are tired of hearing about it.*

9. *Do you want the number of my friend at the F.B.I. who works with the Witness Protection Program?*

10. *Do you think maybe, just maybe, you are an enabler?*

11. *Do you think that possibly you are a mite co-dependent?*

12. *Do you know you have your head in a place where the sun don't shine?*

You have to ask him/her if it's O.K. to go shopping with a friend.

You plan your escape from the relationship/marriage every waking minute, like a house cat eyeing birds outside in the trees.

They are jealous of your family and resent time you spend with your mother, father, sisters, brothers, cousins, aunts, uncles, nieces, nephews, grandpa, grandma, great grandpa, great grandma.

When you run errands, go to the car wash, go to the grocery store, visit your relatives, to the bank, to Starbuck's ALONE . . . you are accused of having an affair.

Whenever you go anywhere alone, you feel like you're being watched or stalked, and most of the time you ARE being watched and stalked.

Your friends, relatives, your boss always start phone conversations with: "Are you alone? Can you talk?"

Your assets (bank accounts, retirement funds, real estate, savings bonds, heirlooms, photos, jewelry, and anything else of value to you) are with trusted friends/relatives or in a safe deposit box.

You do not look forward to YOUR vacations because he/she is going with you to a destination of THEIR choice.

He/she always screens all calls or answers the phone on the first ring . . . including your cell phone if you unwittingly leave it on the kitchen counter.

Whenever you DO talk on the phone, he/she makes sure he/she is always in the room . . . listening, and he/she makes editorial comments in the background about the conversation you are having.

You envy prisoners in jail who have more privacy and phone privileges than you do.

You feel unintelligent and insignificant after spending time with him/her.

They are jealous of your pets and resent time you spend with them.

They are jealous of your friends and resent time you spend with them.

They are jealous of your children and resent time you spend with them.

They are jealous of your job and resent the time you spend at work.

They are jealous of your past—especially friends you had, including former lovers, husbands, wives, aunts, uncles, etc.

They are jealous of your old high school or college yearbooks, photo albums, old personal and special papers, awards, and "accidentally" throw them out on trash day, claiming they thought they were boxes of worthless books and papers.

They are jealous of your education.

They are jealous of any talents or skills you may have that they don't.

They cause you to eat vast amounts of comfort food after an encounter with them, or lose your cookies for the same reason.

They time your trips to the grocery store and check the cash register receipt to see what time you left the store and how long it took you to get home with their dinner.

They are jealous of your personality.

They give you migraines after you have spent time with or talked to them on the phone.

Their constant putdowns (often in front of others) make you feel like crying.

They are jealous of your retirement fund and constantly remind you that if you split from them, they get half of your retirement.

They are jealous of your relatives, especially if you have more brothers and sisters than they have.

They are jealous of your car, especially if it is newer, more expensive, or cleaner than theirs.

They are jealous of the time you spend washing and servicing your car.

They are jealous of the time you spend alone—in and out of your car.

They are jealous of the time you spend watering and pruning your plants.

They are jealous of the furniture you owned before you met them.

They are jealous of your lunch break at work, because it's longer than theirs.

They are jealous of the time you spend running THEIR errands, but keep in close contact by calling your cell phone every 15 minutes.

They are jealous of the auto mechanic, check-out clerk, food server, drive—through teller, sanitary engineers, lawn service, carpenters, plumbers and other contractors, receptionists, your secretary, your employer, your customers, the dog groomer, your minister, salespeople, parking attendants, your doctor, your dentist or any driver you glance at while sitting in traffic.

They are jealous of your job, and they would really prefer that you quit even though you are supporting them with your income.

They make fun of you and call you nasty names and when you react negatively they say they were only kidding around and wonder why, "you can't take a joke?"

They treat you with respect in public, but in private, they depersonalize you and make you feel insignificant.

They make you emotionally constipated: You are at a loss for words in their presence because they constantly intimidate you.

Your friends have:

Contacted a lawyer for you,

found you a new place to live,

researched and summarized all the divorce laws for your state,

created a list of people you can date once you are free,

invested heavily in self-help books for you to read,

bought you every "Hang in There" card ever printed,

and sent in a tape to Dr. Phil for you . . .

Your partner's children want YOU to have custody of them.

Your partner's children want you to move far away, and take them with you . . .

Your partner gives away or sells your pets while you are away; he/she says, "This will save us both money."

They try to convince you to cancel your visitation or time you spend with your children.

They tell lies about you to your relatives, friends, children, employer, and anyone who will listen—behind your back.

They systematically eliminate all your relationships with others because others—friends, relatives, co-workers—don't want to spend time with you because of him/her.

They systematically eliminate all your relationships with other people because they believe that all the love and attention you need is what they shower you with.

They keep reminding you how lucky you are to have them in your life.

They keep reminding you that you will miss them if the two of you ever break up.

They tell you that no one else will ever love you like they do . . . and you are relieved.

On occasion, your partner has thrown things, sometimes AT you, such as a crescent wrench, lamp, chair, plate, beer bottle, fireplace poker, pet, to emphasize a point.

Your partner uses drugs, alcohol, rage, threats to leave; he/she also threatens to harm you, your pets, your children, your possessions or your finances to keep control of you.

He/she says that YOU need to see a counselor to deal with your oversensitivity, anger, nervousness, stress . . .

They want you to take Prozac, Zoloft, eat St. John's Wort, so you can cope with their outbursts, unhealthy habits, their relatives, their job, their kids, their exes.

Their needs are the only legitimate ones. You need therapy to get over yours.

They insist on a joint counseling session, so they can control and monitor what you say to a counselor.

They pit the counselor against you and are satisfied that, "Now things can really work out if we just work together and communicate."

Your partner insists he/she does not have a drinking problem, yet their main food groups are beer, wine, Jack Daniels, and more beer, wine, and Jack Daniels.

You dread spending time with them because they negate almost everything you say or do.

You dread spending time with them because they are verbally abusive, condescending, and have an air of superiority toward you.

You would rather have a root canal than spend any more time with them—ever.

Your life is more complicated and miserable than any soap opera.

You decide you need to write a book, like this one, to relieve stress and make sense of it all.

You receive all your subscriptions, personal mail, bank statements, personal phone calls, e-mail and catalogs at work or at a P. O. Box in the next town.

You go on vacation with your partner (to a location of his/her choosing) and he/she insists on reading all post cards you have written to friends or relatives.

You write all your checks, letters, e-mail at work.

Your cell phone bill is $600.00 a month because you have to make all your private calls from your office, your car, your friends' homes, the vegetable section at the supermarket.

You wish you had never met your partner.

You wonder why God made Hitler, mosquitoes, termites, roaches, Osama Bin Laden, your partner.

Once again, you come away feeling devalued after spending time with him/her.

Your partner reminds you daily that he/she would kill themselves or die (from spite) if you ever left. You hum: "Thank God and Greyhound you're gone."

Your partner constantly reminds you how much you will miss them when they are gone.

You give them a CD of Paul Simon's "Fifty Ways To Leave Your Lover" and hope they take it to heart.

You frequently question your judgment because you have lost all confidence that your mind ever worked since you got involved with this person.

You can only think in your car or in the bathroom stalls at work.

Your family threatens to disown you if you do not leave him/her or get a divorce.

Your family offers to pay for your divorce.

His/her family offers to pay for your divorce.

You keep all your important stuff that won't fit in a Safe Deposit Box—checkbook, change of clothes, passport, receipts, tax returns, etc . . . in your office, or the trunk of your car.

You have dry heaves/get a migraine when they tell you they took the day off to be with you.

They have screamed at you: "If you can't say something nice to me, just SHUT UP, just SHUT THE HELL UP!"

Your energy is constantly sapped after spending time with him/her.

Your divorce attorney gets an order of protection for him/herself, hires a bodyguard, and moves to Yuma, Arizona . . . in August.

Your partner tricks you into taking a long shower, getting a massage, or sends you to the gift shop of your vacation hotel, so they can search your belongings and read your postcards.

You throw spectacular birthday parties for them, their kids, their relatives, their friends; you buy them elaborate gifts . . . and they treat your birthday like it's a nuisance.

You always have to order the entrée of their choice from the menu so they can taste your dinner. You, of course, get stuck eating theirs—a food you detest or that makes you pop Prilosec tablets like they are M & M's.

When you grocery shop, you have to buy all their favorite foods, but there's no money left over for any of yours. The groceries and the mortgage are YOUR financial responsibilities.

You live in a ten-room house you bought before you met, you pay all the bills, yet you cannot decorate any of the rooms in your taste, your children have no place to stay IF they are allowed to visit you, and your friends and relatives are NEVER welcome, especially for the holidays . . .

You have taped/videotaped/have considered taping/videotaping conversations with them to show your shrink, your lawyer, Jerry Springer, Dr. Phil, Oprah.

Your partner turns on the charm whenever you make concrete plans to leave them. They promise for the thousandth time to change their ways if you will only give them one more chance.

Your partner agrees to go for counseling and after three sessions they come home, announce that their counselor has pronounced them 'cured', and start making plans for your "new" future with the "new them."

Your doctor, pharmacist, psychologist, 911 and your mother are on speed dial.

Your weekly intake of Prozac, kava kava, St. John's Wort, valium and Old Bushmill's could tranquilize a buffalo.

Whenever you go someplace, you can bet your cell phone will ring within the hour . . . they hunt you down like a pig hunts down truffles.

You consider committing a crime, such as robbing a Mini-Mart, so you can go to prison for some peace and quiet and limited contact with your partner. Also, you'd get to see your kids, relatives, and friends more often. Because you can add them to your visitors list.

You hope and pray he/she will leave YOU and pay all legal expenses.

You get a P.O. box; your work address is your voter registration address and has been for all the years you have been planning your escape. You have a hard time remembering your REAL address because just like your home phone number, you have hardly ever used it.

When he/she pees, everyone else pees. On long road trips you are not allowed to go to the bathroom when YOU need to go. This rule applies to all passengers, including children and pets.

When travelling by air, he/she insists that you sit by the window so that they can control your movements on the plane and keep you from talking to whomever sits beside you on the aisle seat.

He/she seeks to destroy all your strengths and good qualities, so no one else will find you attractive.

You always use your American Express card to pay for airline tickets, rental cars, hotels, camp sites, hiking trailhead parking, gasoline, etc., and they promise to pay you for their share . . . later, always later.

If not married to him/her, you are still expected to co-sign on credit cards, car loans, mortgages, etc., because they have screwed up their credit.

They announce they are declaring bankruptcy as soon as they convince you to co-sign on a credit card, which they max out in one month.

Your partner insists they are "born again" and GOD will get you if you leave them.

When on vacation or on a business trip or while attending a convention and he/she is with you, he/she is jealous of the concierge, the bell hop, the check-in clerk because they are too friendly towards you.

If you put the milk, O.J., or any other beverage back into the refrigerator with the label out of alignment with other stuff, they lecture you on your lack of organizational skills and slovenliness.

He/she often demands to know what you are thinking—a penny for your thoughts—and if you tell them, they proceed to pick apart your thoughts.

If you refuse to share your thoughts with them, they sull up like a two year old.

They are jealous that you have thoughts without them.

They show up unannounced at your job.

They claim they are worried about your safety and that's why they are sitting on your car when you come out of the grocery store, health spa, your job.

They call your friends when you are not at home to try to weasel information from them that can be used against you.

He/she hovers over you like a mosquito when you are sending or reading YOUR e-mail, or writing on YOUR computer.

He/she flirts with other people to try to make you jealous.

They call you from the local firing range to let you know they are taking lessons.

He/she applies for a job at your company . . . in your department . . . and THEY'RE HIRED; their new boss suggests that the two of you share an office since you're so close anyway!

PART TWO

You Know You Are OUT of a Toxic Relationship When . . .

. . . you can finally go to the grocery store freely.

. . . your ex tells you that if you will only tell him/her where you live he/she promises not to stalk you or your new boyfriend/girlfriend/husband/wife any more.

. . . you can receive phone calls, mail, bank statements, etc. at your home address.

. . . no one knows where you live except the police department that patrols your new neighborhood.

. . . you start a Block Watch and distribute photos of your ex-partner to all your neighbors, the mail carrier, and the police department.

. . . your favorite possessions are your new pit bull, your .22 magnum, and your new motion-sensing spotlights and siren security system.

. . . you have watched "Home Alone" at least six times and have taken notes.

. . . you gladly MOVE to a place you always said, "it would be a cold day in hell before you would ever visit" and the National Weather Service says there's a blizzard in Phoenix."

. . . your friends can finally sleep at night.

. . . you can finally sleep with both eyes closed, without the lump of your personal effects and a pistol under your pillow.

. . . you can finally wear clothes that flatter you in colors of your choice.

. . . you can decorate your new residence in your taste only.

. . . you don't need your P.O. box anymore, except for correspondence from your ex's attorney.

. . . your cell phone is a source of comfort for your ex . . . they call it 20 times a day just to hear your voice and leave whiney/threatening/begging apologies for you.

. . . THEY send cards, flowers, gifts to your office address.

. . . they beg you to give them your new address and home phone number.

. . . they finally get religion . . . and it's YOURS!

. . . they buy a Bible and regale you with Scripture verses on "forgiveness."

. . . They become Biblical scholars to make YOU feel guilty for not tolerating any more of their abusive personality.

. . . they start to teach relationship classes at your church to win you back.

. . . they threaten to find someone else to take your place once and for all. You worry about the stranger's well-being.

. . . they read numerous books on how to make relationships work and try to share them with you.

. . . they start quoting from Robert Schuller and other televangelists to impress you and try to make you feel guilty for isolating yourself from their abuse.

. . . you can buy and eat what you want; you can order your choice of entrée from any menu.

. . . they claim they have changed in merely four days/ three counseling sessions . . . would you please give them another chance (another ten years of your life)?

. . . their "new and improved" personality is REALLY making you sick!

. . . you file an order of protection when you receive a letter from them at your new home address in which they describe your window coverings and the interior of your new house.

. . . YOUR relatives finally see you for the holidays for the first time in many years.

. . . your shrink/attorney/pharmacist have to file bankruptcy; they can't make it without your financial support.

. . . you feel excited to be alive again, and you're only at the laundromat doing just YOUR laundry!

. . . you save so much money on prescription drugs, counseling, attorney's fees, and medical bills, you can finally afford the home of your dreams, a cabin in the woods, AND a summer home by the seashore.

. . . you can get subscriptions and catalogues at home, and buy what you want on E-Bay, or anywhere else without a battle or guilt.

. . . your friends can talk to you about THEIR problems, and you have time and energy to listen.

. . . you realize how sunny it is when your "head is no longer lodged where the sun don't shine."

. . . you can play golf, fish, write, read, walk your dog/play with your cat/ride your horse. And you know you can do this again tomorrow if you wish.

. . . you can use your fitness club membership without fear of being stalked around the weight machines or in the parking lot.

. . . you care about your health because you WANT to live . . . mostly you want to make up for lost time.

. . . you lose that extra stress fat; your body fat percent goes from 30% to 7% in six months.

. . . your children, friends, and relatives want to visit you at your home.

. . . you are content with your material existence, even though you left all your worldly possessions in your former house/garage with him/her just so you could get away.

. . . you no longer need rental storage units (another savings!).

. . . you receive dozens of books, and cards on forgiveness and relationships at work from your ex.

. . . You receive an overload of voice messaging at work from your ex; the overload of messages causes a major system crash for your employer.

. . . you pray your ex finds a new partner/obsession SOON.

. . . you can buy music. You hook up your stereo/CD player for the first time since you met your ex.

. . . you can listen to your music without headphones; there's no one to annoy anymore with classical or other tasteful music.

. . . you can watch television programs you like.

. . . your ex wants to "make amends to your children/family/ friends" he/she always despised and treated abusively.

. . . he/she writes letters of apology to everyone they can think of . . . it takes them several months to complete their list and they make sure you get a copy of every single letter they have written.

. . . your parish priest has to take a coffee break/lunch break to make it through your ex's confession/counseling session.

. . . your ex threatens to kill you if you don't come back . . . because he/she loves you.

. . . your ex threatens to harm your family if you don't come back . . . because he/she loves you.

. . . your ex threatens to commit suicide if you don't come back. You suggest he/she dial 9-1-1. You send him/her a list of the most successful and popular methods and directions to the Golden Gate Bridge.

. . . you can play golf again without packing a pistol in your bag.

. . . you can talk to any food server without fear of reprisal.

. . . you can leave a healthy tip without getting a lecture on wasting money on lazy and incompetent waiters and waitresses.

. . . you buy yourself new underwear, decent shampoo, a new comb . . . without having to show the receipts, or justify WHY you need new undergarments (after only six years.)

. . . you can hang anything you want to over the fireplace, including moose antlers that have been in storage for ten years.

. . . you can visit friends any hour of the day or night.

. . . friends can visit you any hour of the day or night, either sex!

. . . you no longer have the feeling a private investigator has been following you.

. . . you no longer feel the need to "lose" a vehicle that's been following you around the grocery store parking lot.

. . . you no longer try to read every license plate number of the vehicles behind you.

. . . you can buy a new car without permission.

. . . your ex gets a face lift, loses 50 lbs., has a personality makeover, finds Jesus, (and anything else you always wanted them to do) in one month.

. . . now that they have found Jesus, you pray they find a new partner—soon.

. . . now that they have found Jesus, they pray you get amnesia and return.

. . . you have time to service and pamper your new vehicle.

. . . you have a new best friend, and it's NOT your shrink.

. . . you can relax, read, nap, watch television, entertain friends, and anything else normal people do, without fear of reprisal.

. . . you don't listen for the key in the lock with your heart in your throat any more.

. . . you are no longer under the protection of the "Endangered Species Act."

. . . people at church ask YOU to pray for THEM for the first time in years.

. . . you no longer hide out in the confessional during Sunday services so that he/she can't find and sit beside you.

. . . girlfriends at work weep with joy that you are finally out.

. . . male friends at work weep with joy that you are finally out.

. . . you get more invitations to do things you always wanted to do.

. . . you can feel good on your birthday without your ex trying to ruin your good mood.

. . . there is food in your refrigerator and kitchen you like to eat, in vast, comforting quantities . . . and it ain't pork rinds and beer.

. . . you don't cry in your car/office/bathroom every day anymore.

. . . you read more books on travel, hobbies, sports, cooking, building the home of your dreams, etc . . . than self-help books.

. . . you donate to Goodwill all leftover copies of "Women/ Men Who Love Too Much" and the do-it-yourself divorce kits you bought and hid each year. Friends stop sending you self-help books for your birthday.

. . . you really, really like Martin Luther King, Jr.'s speech . . . "free at last, free at last! thank God Almighty, I'm free at last."

. . . you LIKE coming home.

. . . you like being home.

. . . your friends like visiting your home.

. . . your pets can no longer be "deported" to other homes.

. . . you can leave your checkbook out where you can find it.

. . . you can leave your mail on the coffee/kitchen table.

. . . only YOU will open mail addressed to you.

. . . you can keep all your tax receipts at home and not in a bank vault or trunk of your car.

. . . you can hang photos of YOUR children, relatives, friends, pets, etc . . . and they won't mysteriously disappear.

. . . your personal library will remain just as you left it when you return from work/vacation/the store.

. . . you no longer have to service all of their children's vehicles you bought or co-signed for.

. . . you no longer have to insure their vehicle, their children's vehicles . . . boats . . . RV's . . . etc . . .

. . . you no longer have to "help" buy houses for their children.

. . . you no longer have to ingratiate yourself to their relatives, friends, co-workers.

. . . you can feel like a human and not like a circus seal EVERY day.

. . . you can take a walk without getting interrogated.

. . . you can buy as many pairs of shoes as you want.

. . . you can buy pets to replace the ones they disposed of

. . . and . . . pets can be in your house once again: HOORAH!

. . . your pets can sleep with you once again.

. . . you can sleep once again.

. . . you don't have to get all the trash out of your car, and sort through it for "incriminating" papers (i.e. personal purchases, lunch receipts, a job offer in the Czech Republic).

. . . your children's friends no longer ask your children if you are out of that horrible relationship yet.

. . . your co-workers no longer see your life as a source of cheap entertainment or gossip.

. . . your friends and family admire you and have great respect for you for taking charge of your life and successfully starting a new life.

. . . some of your friends, relatives, and coworkers secretly envy what you have done and hope to do it themselves before it's too late.

. . . your sphincter muscle no longer tightens up when your cell phone rings because he/she is no longer controlling you.

. . . you no longer swear like a drunken sailor like you did when you were around this person; the 'F' word is no longer in your vocabulary.

. . . and finally . . . you ask other people the time-honored question:

. . . WHEN are you going to send YOUR tape to Dr. Phil?

THE END!

ABOUT THE AUTHORS

Cage Riley, IV

Cage Riley, IV has been a college professor for thirty-four years and has taught journalism, photography, screenwriting, film, literature, magazine article writing, and numerous personal writing classes during his career; today he teaches personal and exploratory writing, memoir writing, and essay writing dealing with personal life goals and dreams.

Riley grew up in an alcoholic family and is an adult child of alcoholics, though he is neither an alcoholic nor a drug user. He also, like most of you out there, has had to deal with numerous toxic relationships during his lifetime.

Bunny Liberty

Bunny Liberty is a native of New York State. Liberty now lives in the Southwest and teaches, among other things, journal writing, memoir writing, humor writing, and small business proposal writing as a full-time college professor.

Liberty has also worked as a professional writer, staff developer, political aide, and horse trainer.

Liberty believes in the healing power of journal writing and sharing our life stories in supportive settings.

NOTE: The authors are working on a sequel to this book and would like to hear from anyone with humorous, and/or serious stories about experiences they have had or have heard about in toxic relationships on the job, with co-workers, or with the boss. Send stories, anecdotes, etc. to: Toxic Relationships . . . , P.O. Box 50935, Phx., AZ 85044. ALL information will remain totally anonymous with NO names, addresses, or geographic locations revealed!

Made in the USA
Monee, IL
19 October 2026

66035044R00066